Milking the Wild Goat

How to Find Land and Set up Your Homestead

Book 2 in the Get Out of the City and Thrive! series

By Robyn Dolan

DISCLAIMER

Thank you for purchasing "Get Out of the City and Thrive! Book 2 – How to Find Land and Set up Your Homestead" I hope you find it enjoyable, entertaining and helpful.

All persons in this book are real, though most of the names have been changed to protect the innocent (me). Some persons are composites of several different individuals, no likeness to one particular person is intended and composites are used merely for the author's convenience in illustrating a point. All information presented in this work is considered correct as of the time of its writing. All information is presented for educational and entertainment purposes only, no warranties are made and author assumes no responsibility or liability for misuse or misunderstanding of this information or damages due to use of information contained in this book.

This book details the author's personal experiences with and opinions about moving out of the city and making major life changes. The author is not licensed or certified to teach or give legal or medical advice. This book is not a substitute for legal, medical or accounting advice from a licensed professional.

This book provides content related to relocation, lifestyle changes and homesteading topics. As such, use of this book implies your acceptance of this disclaimer.

DEDICATION

TO MY DAD, BOB SIEMANN. YOU WERE THE ANSWER TO A LITTLE GIRL'S PRAYERS, MY BIGGEST CHEERLEADER, AND MY SAFE HARBOR. I LOVE YOU ALWAYS.

ACKNOWLEDGEMENTS

So many people help to write a book. First and foremost, thanks be to God, for the inspiration and constant unrest until I am doing what (I hope) He seems to want. To Yak, for putting up with mom's writing moods and learning curves. To Maryruth and Charles, for never letting up in encouraging me to write and plow into the book business. To my older children, for not putting me in the psych ward. Yet. To Jonah for, keeping me young. To my parents, for not being overly disappointed that I did not choose law or medicine as my vocation. To the folks at Grit Magazine, for letting me in as one of their reader bloggers back in 2008, and occasionally using my work in their publications.

GET OUT OF THE CITY AND THRIVE!

BOOK 2 – MILKING THE WILD GOAT

HOW TO FIND LAND AND SET UP YOUR HOMESTEAD

BOOK 2 – MILKING THE WILD GOAT

HOW TO FIND LAND AND SET UP YOUR HOMESTEAD

GET OUT OF THE CITY AND THRIVE!

BOOK 2 – MILKING THE WILD GOAT

HOW TO FIND LAND AND SET UP YOUR HOMESTEAD

Introduction

Many people dream, at one time or another, of leaving the city and enjoying a "simpler" life in the country. Many of these never pursue that dream. If it is because of fear, set that aside. It is very doable. The process and timing are not the same for everyone who attempts this. But the basics are. I outlined how I did it in Book 1 of this series: Get Out of the City and Thrive – How I did it and How You Can, Too!, which is available on Amazon, Mrs. D's Homestead.com, or your favorite online retailer.

In a nutshell: get the family on board, make a financial plan, start making the adjustments to your lifestyle and set a date. Investigate the areas you are interested in, ways to make a living in those areas and whether you can achieve the lifestyle you are aiming for there – more about making a living in Book 3: Get Out of the City and Thrive - Paying for the Dream – How to Thrive on Your Homestead.

If you are reading this book, I am assuming you have read Get Out of the City and Thrive - Book 1: How I did it and How You Can, Too! and are ready to start seriously looking for land, or are ready to start setting up your homestead. So let's get on with it!

"THE FIRST AND MOST IMPORTANT THING TO DO, WHEN YOU'RE READY TO PURSUE THE HOMESTEADING LIFESTYLE IS TO LEARN SOME BASIC SKILLS. EDUCATE YOURSELF."

Playing Pretend

When I was growing up we didn't have much. Mom was a widow and had to work full-time to support Grandma and me. We made do and saved hard. Grandma cooked from scratch and Mom baked a half-dozen loaves of bread every month. They sewed all of our clothes. Mom's hard-earned dollars and grandma's ingenuity bought us a cozy little bungalow in the suburbs and from there, I learned how to live.

I took a great interest in sewing and needlework and mom and grandma patiently taught me. At the age of five I had my own little sewing box with needles, embroidery floss and hoops, scissors, and little iron-on patterns. I had the greatest struggle learning french knots. Then, when I thought I had it down, mom would challenge me to the next level – making the stitches more even, then making the design look the same on both the front and the back of the fabric. Grandma was always knitting for us – socks, mittens, caps. I couldn't seem to get both of my hands working together with the knitting needles, so she taught me how to crochet. I learned with gusto. Soon I was crocheting afghans. But to a nine year old an afghan takes an eternity, so mine would get put aside for months at a time.

I think I was twelve when I finally got to learn to sew on a sewing machine. Mom was hesitant to let me use hers or grandma's, so they found an old Singer treadle machine. A treadle machine does not require electricity. It is entirely mechanical. The needle is moved up and down by rocking a pedal back and forth with the feet. This turns a large wheel which is connected by a leather belt to a smaller hand wheel on the sewing machine, which moves the needle up and down through the fabric. Grandma cleaned and oiled the old machine and made a new leather belt for it out of an old men's belt. Finally I was seated at the sewing machine. Mom showed me over and over how to thread it. I would be pedaling along, sewing seams, having a great time, when suddenly the thread would break and I would get lost somewhere in the directions and have to go get mom. It's still happening thirty years later. My mom stays up with every new-fangled sewing machine that comes out and I'm still trying to remember how to thread the treadle or grandma's old factory model Pfaff properly. It's okay, I know how to turn my computer on, mom still needs help.

I loved to go to the store with dad (mom remarried

when I was 8) and do my embroidery or crochet on the way, pretending we were going visiting to the neighbor's farm. On our yearly vacation we would actually visit farms of relatives and friends in various parts of the Midwest – Minnesota, North Dakota, South Dakota, Tennessee or Indiana. Once we visited a dairy farm. The Holstein milk cows looked about ten feet tall, lined up in their milking parlors. Now that was intimidating! For all my daydreaming, I wasn't quite ready for the mud and the bugs and the humidity of farming. Or the WORK!!

Dad built me a play loft in the garage and I would spend hours up there watching him putter with his woodworking projects down below, pretending I was in the loft of the "Little House on the Prairie". I loved watching my dad work. I loved the smell of freshly sawn wood. Among my dad's many projects, he built a sturdy workbench which is still in use nearly forty years later, by my sons, and frequently, me. He built a large wardrobe lined with cedar, which mom used to use for changing out summer and winter wardrobes. Now she has a scaled down wardrobe and the old closet mostly stores extra coats. My parents are great music lovers, something they passed on to me, and they had amassed a large collection of vinyl LP's before CD's and MP3's made them obsolete. Dad built a large record cabinet that still stands, polished and pretty, in the family room. Though it only gets opened and closed anymore when someone pulls a record to transfer to an MP3 file.

I took woodshop in summer school one year. I actually made a wooden spoon that saw many years of good use, and a wooden candy dish, shaped like a spade – the kind you see on playing cards. Later I tried my hand at refinishing furniture, with some success, if I could manage to come up with the money for varnish.

Almost every year Dad and I would plant a little garden in the back yard. Well, I liked the idea of the garden, but Dad did most of the work. I would occasionally water, and frequently gaze at the garden, but mostly Dad was the one who got the stuff growing. I loved watching the tomatoes form and ripen. I loved pulling up the first radishes and the few carrots. I confess, I did not properly appreciate swiss chard and beet greens in those early years. I liked buttery soft greenleaf lettuce and crunchy iceberg lettuce, anything with a bit more flavor was just too strong for me. I always made sure my salads had plenty of salad dressing and that any cooked greens were smothered in butter, salt and pepper.

One year we added on to our house. Where the screened in patio with the block barbeque and the laundry room were, there was to be a large family room with open beam ceilings. Dad got to add detail to the beams with a router and then stain and varnish them before they went up. A fireplace was also added. This extended the house out over much of what used to be my back yard play area. The clotheslines went away, along with the swingset. I got a taste of what it would be like to have friends and family all working together to build a home. Later, when dad built me a playhouse, mom and I went shopping for material and I learned how to make curtains for the windows. I also helped roof and paint the playhouse and a couple of years later, the garage and house. I loved learning to do these things. It gave me a sense of confidence that I could do some things for myself.

So, you see, I developed quite an appreciation for hand built, do it yourself projects. The first and most important thing to do, when you're ready to pursue the homesteading lifestyle is to learn some basic skills. Educate yourself.

"Whether you start with bare land, or buy something "turn-key" (real estate-ese for "ready to move in"), homesteading is a lifelong, ongoing project."

Getting Ready to Set Up

Setting up a homestead is not a quick and easy process. Whether you start with bare land, or buy something "turn-key" (real estate-ese for "ready to move in"), homesteading is a lifelong, ongoing project. There are three basic ways to go, when getting started:

Buying bare land and living in an RV, truck camper, or trailer.

Buying bare land and building from scratch, possibly camping on the property while doing so.

Buying land with existing structures and renovating and reusing them.

"One of the easiest ways to get started on your homestead is to live in an RV."

Living in an RV

One of the easiest ways to get started on your homestead is to live in an RV. Whether this is a motorhome, travel trailer, or truck camper, if you have solar panels and/or a generator, it is merely an issue of refilling your propane tanks as necessary, refilling your fresh water and dumping your waste water. This is easily enough accomplished by driving in to the nearest facility to dump and refill (rv park, truck stop, or other sanitation station). You will want to learn and apply some serious water conservation skills to make this less of a hassle.

You will also probably want to make these some of the first issues you address at your homestead. If you don't have a way to recharge your "house" batteries, you may want to look at getting the electricity hooked up, first. Having said that, I cannot overemphasize the feeling of freedom that comes with being off-grid. I would highly recommend solar panels and a generator. Or at least having your trailer or camper wired to recharge off of your engine alternator. Just remember to unplug once the batteries are charged, so they don't continue to drain your vehicle battery. Also, keep in mind that some appliances will need an inverter, to convert DC to AC power, and in some cases, extra battery power for these appliances.

There are other options to address the issues of heating, water and electricity on your homestead, and numerous books and websites devoted to the subject, both on and off-grid. You can find some of them in the *Resource* section at the back of this book. In the coming chapters, I will relate how we resolved these important life necessities as we started out on our homestead, and thoughts about other alternatives.

The last thing I will say here, about RV living, is that you have your house all set up. Yes, you are living on a smaller scale than in a "sticks-and-bricks" home, but you have your refrigerator, stove, oven, microwave, bathroom, comfortable beds, and shelter from the elements. You are also not tied to a specific location, so if you are not careful, you could become addicted to the RV lifestyle. On the other hand, it will be easy-peasy to take a trip, or go camping after you get your homestead set up.

"Sadly, there is no place that is untouched by building restrictions. Just think of it as a necessary evil — you wouldn't want your neighbor to dump his waste just anywhere, especially if you have to smell it..."

Building from Scratch

Starting with unimproved land can be very exciting. Building exactly what you want, how you want is a wonderful option. Especially if you have done your homework and gotten land in an unincorporated area, with the fewest restrictions possible. Sadly, there is no place that is untouched by building restrictions. Just think of it as a necessary evil – you wouldn't want your neighbor to dump his waste just anywhere, especially if you have to smell it, or if it ends up draining onto your property. Yuck! Everybody has different standards of hygiene.

If you intend to build from scratch, without living on the property while you are building, and especially if you hire someone else to do it, make sure you are supervising every step of the way. A contractor who gets mad at you for checking up every few days is one that you especially need to keep tabs on. You can read about my experience with that in the chapter about "The House".

When you are starting with vacant land, you are going to need permits and inspections before and after every part of the build. You cannot just start wherever you want. Each building department has its own rules about what comes first in a residential dwelling. If you are a horse person, you will probably be fencing and building the barn or some outbuildings first, so check to make sure that this will work for you. If you are planning to live on the property while building, some areas have restrictions on this and some simply do not allow it. Make sure you check. Even better, check on all this before you buy. You will have enough surprises, even if you have carefully researched everything you think you need.

"There are quite a few pros and cons to starting with land that includes existing structures. If one of them is a home you have 4 walls and a roof over your head. And hopefully your hot and cold running water works."

Existing Structures

There are quite a few pros and cons to starting with land that includes existing structures. Primarily, if one of them is a home, even if it is not brand new, you have 4 walls and a roof over your head. You will probably have ongoing repairs and upgrades to contend with and you might want to change everything around, but it is something to start with. And hopefully your hot and cold running water works.

Existing structures can also include storage sheds, barns, pasture shelters (anything critters can stand or sit under to get out of the elements), pump houses (for wells and cisterns), garages, warehouse buildings, etc.

Another advantage to starting with an improved property is that most or all of your "infrastructure" may already be there:

Water systems – co-op; tank and pump; well and pump; cisterns, filters and pump.

Sewage systems – sewer hook-ups; cesspool; septic; leach fields.

Electrical systems – grid hook-ups; solar/wind system; generator.

Heating systems – natural or propane gas; wood stoves or fireplaces; passive solar heat; recirculating heat (under floor).

Some disadvantages are:

Constant repairs: as with anything used, expect to always be fixing something. If you're lucky and smart, you can stay one step ahead of the next breakdown.

Hidden problems: again, buying used means relying on your eyes, ears, nose (foul smells) and your expertise to flush out potential problems. Foundations crumble, termites and other critters hide in walls, leaky roofs only leak after it starts raining, etc.

Unpermitted repairs/remodels/construction: such items will add hassle and expense when you go to get a permit for *your* remodel/repair/addition. It is not pleasant to find you have to do a major alteration to your house, just to get a permit for the garage you want to build. If you decide to check with the local building department about a property you do not own, be discreet. Having the building department pay a surprise visit to your seller's property can make him less amenable to your offer.

The Land

I highly advocate buying cheap land and setting up your own homestead, according to your preferences. However, I advise anyone considering this to proceed with caution. If land is cheap, there is a reason for it.

"Never underestimate the importance of water and sanitation facilities."

Camp

In my case, it was the lack of water, the remote location, and the lack of services in the area. Never underestimate the importance of water and sanitation facilities. Electricity can be provided by solar panels, generators or wind. Where we ended up, it was not prohibitive to hook up to the grid, as the electric lines were located near enough to my property. We also installed a propane tank and signed up for propane delivery. We could have gotten by with small, portable tanks that we could take in to town to refill, if we had chosen to go that route.

As time has gone by, cellular and internet service has greatly improved in our area. But every drop of water has to be hauled in by us or a water delivery truck. This is not so bad for just washing, drinking and cooking. But for gardening and livestock, it is very expensive.

Luckily, our parcel "perked" for a septic system. This means that the ground was absorbent enough to put in leach lines and a septic tank for gray and black water. Alternative waste disposal systems in this area are either very expensive, or not approved by the building authorities.

Even rural communities have building and zoning codes, whether or not they are enforced. Life can become very uncomfortable when you are fighting for your right to build the type of home you want. It is best to investigate local zoning and building requirements, land characteristics and water availability. Also road maintenance, if that is a concern to you. Our dirt road is a school bus route, so it is well maintained, but we have several friends who are not so fortunate. They either get washed out or must maintain their own roads throughout the year. Roads that aren't maintained can be very hard on vehicles and passengers alike. If one of your neighbors doesn't have a grader to smoothe down the road, it can also get very expensive to hire one.

Another detail that can seem like a pain, but can actually be somewhat important is to check out your professionals. When I bought my property, I just wanted to get the set-up done quickly and get to living life. I ended up fighting my real estate agent, contractor and others for specific performance. Buyer beware is not a comfortable situation to be in. You should be comfortable and feel able to trust in your agents and contractors. Sadly, this is not always the case. Do not be afraid to shop around for a real estate agent, contractor, finance broker and title company that you have confidence in.

After a couple of false starts, we acquired five acres in the high desert (about fifty-eight hundred feet up) with lots of juniper trees, and a "seasonal stream" cutting across the back.

Here we set down the camper and pitched the tents and acquired a "package". First we purchased the land, then our agent set us up with a contractor, (neither of whom I will name, to protect my innocence) who obtained an old, broken down double-wide trailer for us and performed "all" the necessary requirements to get us hooked up and living in it, such as digging and installing the septic tank, installing a 2500 gallon fresh water tank and the plumbing to get the water into the "house", hooking us up to the grid for electricity and getting the final "green" tag from the county. As I will relate, this did not go smoothly at all.

"Not having very much confidence in my architectural skills, but certain I could put together a kit, we went to Sears and purchased one."

The Shed

Our first project, before we began moving all our possessions out of storage and to our new home was to erect an eight foot by ten foot storage shed. Not having very much confidence in my architectural skills, but certain I could put together a kit, we went to Sears and purchased one. On the way home, we picked up some cinder blocks and 2x4s cut to the kit's specifications for a "foundation". We built the foundation with very little fanfare. Figuring out how to erect the shed was a little more challenging. Suffice it to say that the directions were not user friendly. After much trial and error, erecting and taking apart and putting back together, we had a shed up. Certain pieces didn't fit right and the roof is still held down by large rocks, but it is still standing. I swore that day, that from then on I would trust to my own ingenuity rather than a cheap kit.

"My favorite times were when we were all together at camp, doing schoolwork, or exploring or just relaxing. It was like an extended camping trip, roasting marshmallows and watching the stars at night. Cowboy coffee in the morning and enjoying or enduring whatever the day might bring."

A Camper and two tents

The land we settled on was a serene 5 acres of juniper trees, algerita berry bushes and dry creek bed. My daughter, the horse person, took one look and said, "This is it, mom". It took me two weeks of walking the property, sitting on it for hours at a time, and contemplating before I said, "It is." We made the offer, and after a minimum of haggling, closed escrow in another two weeks.

Getting our double-wide trailer – our house – set up on our five acres was an ordeal. From the time we signed papers with the contractor, to our move-in date was approximately 3 months. My big mistake during that time was not checking up on the contractor on a daily basis. I trusted that he would get his job done. As our move-in date neared, we gave notice on our lease, packed our lives into boxes once again and began moving everything to our new storage shed on the property, where we found – nothing. I called our agent. He said I would have to deal with the contractor. I called the contractor. After clarifying to him what I expected, he commenced to finish the job I had contracted him for.

Suffice it to say that it took him another 2 months to finally fulfill his contract and even then, we had to call the plumbers and electricians back so many times that I finally just did most of the repairs myself.

We parked the camper, relieving the pick-up of that particular burden, in favor of a 425 gallon water tank in the truck bed. We chose a central spot where our two tents would be sheltered by the camper and several trees. We dug a shallow fire pit and outlined it with rocks. Our large cooler was placed nearby. We filled our new shed with boxes of books, papers and more perishable items. The furniture we set in the shelter of more trees and covered it with tarps.

My daughter and I slept in one of the tents, my youngest son and the dogs in the other, and my oldest son in the camper. I know this may sound odd, but I figured I could keep track of him better if he had to make some noise getting out of the camper, than if he was able to sneak out of a tent. Meals were usually cooked over our fire pit, though occasionally in the camper kitchen. Our tiny 3-way fridge (propane, electric, DC) was supplemented by the large cooler, which we had to buy ice for several times a week.

Our shower was a work of art. We hung a 5 gallon solar shower on the east facing wall, outside of the camper, so that by about 10a.m., the water was the perfect temperature for a shower. Using a tall stepladder for one corner and to hold our towels, soap, etc, and a tree branch for another corner, we draped old sheets all around a little wash tub in which the bather would stand. Short, quick showers were the order of the day, but they felt oh, so good! And usually the sun and a gentle breeze dried us before we were done.

Days were very hot, and frequently windy. Nights were getting cold. I was working in Williams, thirty miles away, a few evenings a week. I would have to take the kids with me. Thank heavens my employers were very understanding, and my children not too disruptive (at least while I was working!).

My favorite times were when we were all together at camp, doing schoolwork, or exploring or just relaxing. It was like an extended camping trip, roasting marshmallows and watching the stars at night. Cowboy coffee in the morning and enjoying or enduring whatever the day might bring.

When the weather grew too chilly to continue sleeping in the tents, my employers kindly gave me a discount on a motel room for a couple weeks.

"If you are offered a 900 square foot home for $3,000, you may want to question – why?"

The House

When our trailer finally arrived, we were anxious to start moving in. The weather extremes had been taxing our endurance for weeks now and after our time at the hotel, we had sought relief in a visit to my parents.

Our used trailer was a condemned double-wide. We found out later that it had been designated "unliveable" by another city, due to age, asbestos insulation, and aluminum electrical wiring. Which leads me to my next recommendation: if you are offered a 900 square foot home for $3,000, you may want to question – why? We blew out nearly every outlet before learning to run only one large appliance at a time. Finally, surviving this ordeal, we settled into our new life.

When our water storage tank arrived and was placed on a level dirt pad, I wanted it buried, but was informed the "the water never freezes around here". Within weeks I had repaired and replaced frozen water pipes at least five times. We were nowhere near any city water hook up. In fact, we were at least 7 miles away, and with no well on our property - the groundwater being over 900 feet down and the cost to drill prohibitive. So we had to put a 400 gallon tank in the back of the pick-up to haul water from the town water station – a hose from the town well which would fill up the hauling tank – then bring it home and pump it from the hauling tank into the storage tank.

Our septic system was finally installed and covered. It was nice to know we would no longer have to worry about falling into the deep holes dug for the perk test and tank. As there was no sewer connection nearby we were required to have some means of disposing of used water from dish washing, laundry, toilet flushing, etc. In a septic system the waste goes through pipes into a holding tank from which the water can leach back into the ground and solids can break down over time without contaminating the surrounding soil, groundwater, etc.

It would be yet another cold, cold month before the propane got hooked up so we could run the forced-air heater and cook on the stove and have hot water through the pipes. In the meantime, we huddled in layers of clothing and blankets around smelly, sooty kerosene heaters, which we were grateful to have, and grateful for the heat they put out. A note on kerosene heaters. Get the proper wick for the heater. I could not find the right one for one of the heaters so I used the one from the other heater, which did not fit properly. One night our dog was frantically running between our rooms trying to awaken us. When I got up I found the heater smoking profusely. I immediately turned it off and opened the windows. When I stopped shaking, I decided we would not use that heater anymore and picked up another electric space heater.

When the electricity was finally turned on, we celebrated by putting up ALL our Christmas lights and decorations. It was December 20th. We could now cook some of our meals in our convection/microwave oven and in the crock pot and electric frypan. We brought in the tiny electric heater and also got an old fridge. Also, with the advent of our electricity, we could plug in the water pump and experience anew the miracle of running water moving through the pipes and into the house, flush toilets, and water in the faucets (albeit, cold water, since the gas water heater was not hooked up yet).

Our telephone was installed shortly after we moved in, so we were excited to hook up the computer and finally get back on the internet. I look back on those days of dialup and just shake my head as I tap my fingers waiting for sites to load with my DSL connection.

Another major benefit of having the electricity on - now we could use our own washing machine instead of going to the laundromat. We were eventually glad for the gas so we could use the dryer, too, but then, as now, I do enjoy hanging clothes outside on the line. An added bonus was not having to go outside to the fire pit to cook our meals and heat up water. We were really looking forward to using the central heating, but the motor would not start. A repairman came and cleaned it and lubricated it and finally we had decent heat in our large new home.

I loved the floor plan of our trailer. Three huge rooms. On each end a huge bedroom and bath and in the middle a wide open kitchen and living room area. It felt so open and rambling. I enjoyed sharing a room with my daughter and hoped the boys would enjoy their large room. If not, we would build a wall down the middle, to give them each their own room.

"We went outside and filled some cans with dirt from the yard and planted some seeds in them. We placed them on the steps in the sun and watered them. Day after day. Week after week."

The Garden (How Does A Garden Grow?)

We were going to grow all our own food. I was pretty good with tomatoes, and managed to get an occasional lettuce leaf. But now we had LAND! We would have dozens of gardens. Flowers, vegetables, secret gardens, water gardens, fields of grass for the animals we would have. One day, as part of our school lessons, we went outside and filled some cans with dirt from the yard and planted some seeds in them. We placed them on the steps in the sun and watered them. Day after day. Week after week. No sprouts ever ventured above the surface of the dirt. We got tired of waiting and went to the grocery store. We later realized that our soil was heavy volcanic clay, liberally populated with rocks. The amazing things that did grow were well adapted to shallow root systems, lack of water and a soil that just would not absorb water. Our gardening attempts were put off for future years.

If you are going to live a subsistence lifestyle and grow all your own food and the food for your animals, or at least the majority of it, make sure your land will support it and that you have plenty of water. Our water table was at least 900 feet down. There was no way I was going to recoup the cost of drilling and maintaining a well to provide water for extensive gardens and grass, livestock and us. The cost of hauling in all that water was not so bad in the winter, but very expensive in time and money in the summer. I did not have the resources to set up drip systems and efficient irrigation systems for my dream of hayfields, flowers, vegetable gardens, orchards and woodlots.

Another consideration is that you may need to hire some help with some of your projects. Our soil may not have been optimal for gardening, but the manure from all our livestock, along with compost materials provided excellent amendments. The problem was that I did not have the upper body strength to dig all this good stuff into the rock hard ground. When I occasionally had someone to help me, the garden would really benefit from the soil amendments. When the monsoon rains came, I was always grateful for a break from hauling water and moving sprinklers and hoses. What we did get out of the garden was usually delicious, but not enough to warrant the cost and labor. I also found that corn did not do so well in my garden. It came out starchy and stunted.

I had not a clue what makes good soil. For me, it was a matter of covering a seed with some dirt and watering. If that didn't work, there was the grocery store. I knew nothing of aeration, fertilizer and when and how much to apply (don't you just sprinkle it on the lawn in the spring and fall with some grass seed and water it once in awhile?). I had never composted or raised earthworms. You would never catch me drinking manure tea. And yet, I had successfully raised dozens of bushels of tomatoes out in California. Not to mention the zucchini, swiss chard and radishes. What I did not take into account was that, despite our 5700' elevation, we were still living in a mainly desert landscape. Our little valley was full of junipers and cacti, yucca and algerita bushes.

Yet, every year I persisted in trying to grow something. I eventually found that I had pretty good luck with potatoes. I discovered that lettuces needed shelter from the debilitating winds and oppressive sun and thrived in a sunny window inside the house and that most everything would grow with lots of water. Almost a full, 425 gallon load extra per day in the dry part of the gardening season. Even the monsoon rains did little to lessen the need to water the garden, though the humidity and cloud cover did seem to perk it up.

"Nothing gets clothes cleaner than a washboard, rainwater and homemade soap."

Laundry

I've tried the washboard a few times. Nothing gets clothes cleaner than a washboard, rainwater and homemade soap. But by the time I get done scrubbing that pair of socks I remember what a blessing electricity is, along with hot and cold running water, indoor plumbing, flush toilets, and a Maytag washing machine. I do like my homemade laundry soap, and of course, the solar (clothesline) dryer.

Then, again, after I've had to re-wash a load because it got blown all over with dirt, I have been known to do a few loads in the gas dryer. Also, when hanging the clothes indoors on a windy or wintry day gets too tedious, it's easy enough to use the dryer. Then there are those days when the laundry doesn't get done until after dark...

There are other ways of doing laundry that don't involve back breaking work or electricity. Several interesting variations of washtub have been tried. My current favorite is a 5 gallon bucket, with a good lid. A (clean) toilet plunger is fitted through a hole in the lid. Water, detergent and clothes are added, the lid locked on and the plunger agitates the clothes (with the help of a human moving the plunger up and down). Dump water, rinse, rinse again. Now there is the issue of wringing out the water. A wringer can be used, or an electric spinner. Either one will extract quite a bit of water from the clothes which can then be dried either on the line or with a small portable dryer. The total cost of this entire setup is less than $200, even if the electrical components are chosen. That sure beats a washboard or a $1500 set of water and gas hogging washer and dryer.

I make my own laundry soap and dryer balls instead of store bought dryer sheets. For one thing, it is more convenient and far less costly than running to the store for detergent. For another thing, I think it is healthier. I make my laundry soap from soap ends and non-saleable bars of my homemade soaps, grated and melted with sodium carbonate, borax and essential oils. For sodium carbonate, I get a big bag of baking soda and bake a few cups of it on cookie sheets, at 400 degrees F for 30 minutes. This changes the sodium bicarbonate into sodium carbonate, the active ingredient in most detergents. Mixed with the melted soap and borax, it gels and makes a nice, soft laundry soap. This soap, mixed with a bit more water, makes a great dish soap. Alternatively, I use my homemade bar soap as a chef's soap for washing dishes, especially when I need more grease-cutting action.

Dryer balls are easy to make and I like them so much better than dryer sheets. I like to have about 4 of them.

They keep the clothes moving in the dryer and help them to dry faster and with fewer wrinkles (if the clothes are removed from the dryer right away). They do not add any toxic chemicals to the clothes or the air and are easily and cheaply made and replaced. Of course, you can pay top dollar for them pre-made, as well, but that is still better than fabric softener or dryer sheets, in my opinion, and they last a good, long time. Here's how I make them, if you want to try. Some people get brand new wool yarn and make them. I go to the thrift stores and look for 100% wool sweaters or blankets and unravel them. Then I roll the yarn into balls, about the size of my fist. These are placed into an old nylon stocking, knotted in between balls. This is thrown in the washer and dryer 4 or 5 times, right along with a load of clothes. After about 4 or 5 wash and dries, the balls are pretty well matted and will not unroll. The knots in the stocking are cut, balls removed and used in the dryer with every load. They don't always remove the static, especially if it is extra windy outside, or there are lots of sweaters and blankets in the load, but they soften, speed drying and prevent static in most regular loads.

This brings me to my next section. Making stuff from scratch.

"The idea of a homestead is to move toward a more self-sufficient, less cash dependent/cash enslaved lifestyle."

Making Stuff From Scratch

The idea of a homestead is to move toward a more self-sufficient, less cash dependent/cash enslaved lifestyle. So I try to make everything possible from scratch. The reality of this is the minute I get the last clean dishes put away the counter is reloaded with dirty dishes again. It seems I spend days on end in the kitchen: grinding grain, baking bread, cooking meals, processing gallons of milk into butter, cheese, yogurt, and ice cream; baking cookies and crackers; frying tortillas; popping popcorn; killing, cleaning, dressing and wrapping chickens, rabbits and fish; making hamburger, sausage and bacon, then cooking it; canning, dehydrating, freezing; sweeping, mopping, washing dishes…it never ends. This is really when I wonder how on earth they did it "back then"?! This is also when I realize without a doubt that I was NOT born into the wrong century. I am grateful for the option to flip a switch for light, buy a loaf of bread if I have just been too busy or the weather too hot to bake, or pull a (homemade) dinner out of the freezer if I'm just too tired to cook. Then I can vegetate in front of the telly, with a big bowl of microwave popcorn and my latest Netflix.

That said, there is a certain satisfaction that comes from doing things from scratch; reusing items that no longer serve their intended purpose, but are not yet ready for the trash bin; making something usable out of junk mail or old clothes or excess packaging. Taking bits of fabric and fashioning them to replace disposable paper and plastic products, such as paper towels, paper napkins, Ziploc bags, plastic wrap or sandwich and snack bags. Finding easier ways to do these things is another advantage of finding like-minded friends. Sometimes it's a matter of getting a few gals together and processing a haul of zucchini into pickles, relish and bread. Other times a look on the internet will reveal a new recipe for sauerkraut that's much less labor intensive than the one I've been using. I have streamlined many of my daily chores just by being open to learning from others who are doing the same things.

Fresh milk straight from the goat or cow is a wondrous, health-giving, vitamin and enzyme packed super food. What to do with the excess is a constant challenge. While extra milk can always be fed back to other animals, it seems a lot of work for such an expensive product to not be used for human consumption. I make yogurt, cheese curds, baked cheese, cream cheese, and soap with my abundance. I have tried making hard cheeses, but I just don't have the right conditions for ageing cheese at this time.

I have gone through several grain grinding methods in my efforts to make the freshest, most nutritious foods for my family. In the end, I burned out an expensive grain grinder, obtained unsatisfactory results from hand grinders and burned up a blender and a coffee grinder trying to get the right consistency for my flour. I find that already milled organic flour saves me the time and frustration and is readily available for a reasonable price almost anywhere. We have also cut way back on our grain consumption, so we don't go through as much flour as we used to.

As I said, I make my bar soap from scratch, with extra goat milk. From this bar soap, I also make laundry soap, stain sticks and dish soap. I also bake baking soda to change its chemical makeup to sodium carbonate – the active ingredient in a popular laundry brightener. It is also the active ingredient in most detergents.

I make or upcycle all our clothing from fabric gotten at a discount, or thrift store finds. My son sometimes gets new t-shirts or a hoodie as a gift. We buy our socks, but they get mended over and over until they simply need to be replaced. Other undies are bought new, as well. Shoes we usually buy new, then try to make them last as long as possible. We wear dollar store flip flops a lot or go barefoot.

I have learned to accept gifts of other people's bounty and to preserve it as quickly as possible.

Cabbage makes great sauerkraut, though we also love to eat it fried. Zucchini makes wonderful pickles, and shredded, it can last quite a while in the freezer, to be added to breads, pancakes and casseroles. Tomatoes get sauced and canned, to be cooked into a variety of sauces, soups and juices. Pumpkins are eaten cooked, juiced (ala "Harry Potter"), and canned for pies and soups. Even the cactus gets harvested. Our prickly pear pads are a bit too prickly for eating, but the fruits are cooked and juiced, straining the cactus spikes out of them. I have made rose petal jam and syrup (good for vitamin C). My dad's lemons and grapefruit are eaten fresh and canned. Every few years the algerita bushes on my property produce berries which are very healthful, but bitter. Sweetening greatly improves their flavor and they make a popular, local jam.

When you decide to live 50 or more miles from "everywhere", it pays to learn how to "use it up, wear it out, make it do, or do without". Grow whatever food you can. Salvage building supplies. Hit the yard sales. Learn to shop less frequently. Keep a month or more supply of food stocked. Learn to cook at least a few things from scratch.

"Be sure to take grazing and water into consideration when you are looking for your land."

The Critters

What homestead would be complete without the addition of animals? Animals for food and companionship are a very sustainable commodity. Especially if they can graze on plants growing on the property. They reproduce themselves, so the initial investment is recouped many times. Excess animals can always be sold to bring in a few dollars. At least on a homestead that actually grows grass and has a source of water that does not have to be hauled in on a daily or weekly basis. If animals are even a remote possibility in your homestead plan, be sure to take grazing and water into consideration when you are looking for your land.

When you consider animals, also take into consideration vet bills, feed, water, shelters, fencing, and protection from predators.

"Our first venture into the raising of livestock was a pair of breeding rabbits who immediately suffered fatal heat stroke after being improperly housed in direct sunlight."

Rabbits

Our first venture into the raising of livestock was a pair of breeding rabbits who immediately suffered fatal heat stroke after being improperly housed in direct sunlight. All was not going according to plan. Obviously I needed to supplement my daydream with some education.

We set up our second set of rabbits in the barn, or as it is technically called, a mare motel. This is basically a big roof on posts, and ours had several stalls set up beneath it. Intended as a shelter for horses, the stall panels were steel posts welded together, with a gate on one side. A person could squeeze through easily without opening the gate. The coyotes quickly discovered this, and spent the first night figuring out how to open the rabbits' cages. Our next day's work was thus set before us, and before night two, we had wrapped the rabbit stall in welded wire and poultry netting, and put up a few plywood panels to keep the coyotes from digging in. This was not to be the end of our travails, for we then proceeded to leave a feed barrel and a workbench right next to the wall outside the stall, which the coyotes found to be an ideal boost to jump the fence into the stall and once again, terrorize our bunnies. Upon second finding of overturned cages and terrified rabbits, we deduced the problem and immediately removed it. No further problem with attacks on the bunnies.

Although many people wince at the thought of eating such cute, furry creatures, and in fact several neighbor children have made it their mission to regularly attempt to "rescue" our bunnies, rabbits are just as important and inexpensive a food source as chickens. They're probably cheaper than chickens, but we like eggs, so we always try to keep both.

I like chicken, but in my opinion, rabbit is a whole lot easier to deal with. You don't have to deal with feather shafts you can't remove, you can cook them in all the same ways, and if you are so inclined, you have a nice, soft pelt you can use in a number of ways. Baby rabbits can also be sold to pet stores, or neighbor children...

"Then tragedy struck...early one morning, our german shepherd mix, Lucky, and rotweiler, Flea, decided to play with the goats. Only goats don't play like dogs."

Milking the Wild Goat

Soon we procured a milk goat from one of our friends and built a pen for her a few feet from the house, with a couple of trees for shade. Jenny was part Nubian and mostly Alpine or Toggenberg, we never found out for sure. But she was a prolific milker. We milked her twice a day and got about a half gallon each time. Shortly after, we acquired a companion and future mate for her, a little buck we named Georgie. He tried to adopt Jenny as his new momma, but she quickly put him in his place.

Then tragedy struck...early one morning, our german shepherd mix, Lucky, and rotweiler, Flea, decided to play with the goats. Only goats don't play like dogs. When I realized the goat was screaming, I flew out of the house, to discover Flea hanging onto Jenny's neck and Georgie apparently dead. I began screaming as loud as I could, but the drawback of being so far out was that no one could hear me. With a surge of adrenaline, I forced Flea's jaws open, dragged him off Jenny and chained him up. Then I chained up Lucky, who had not yet gotten hold of her, and went to assess Jenny's wounds. She had a bleeding, gaping hole in her neck, and several other bites, which due to their nature, I decided needed immediate veterinary attention. I lifted her into the truck and turned to face the dead kid. But now I could see him breathing, and looking around. I went and cradled Georgie in my arms, sobbing, and checked him for injuries. It seems he went into the best defense a small animal has against an attacker. Play dead and hope it leaves you alone. Jenny must have drawn the dogs away from him. It would not be the last time she sacrificed herself for the herd.

Not knowing what else to do with Georgie for the moment, I loaded him in the truck with Jenny and phoned the vet, who was not even in yet, to tell him that we were coming in with an emergency. It would take us 45 minutes to drive from our homestead to the nearest veterinary clinic, in Chino Valley. On the way I decided the dogs had to go to the pound. I could not have my own animals killing each other for sport.

The vet was aghast at Jenny's injuries and took her straight into surgery. Georgie was kept near her, just because of the shock he had suffered. A couple of her bites were disinfected and stitched, and her worst injury, where Flea was dragging her by the neck, was fitted with a drain, a finger of a latex glove, open on both ends, which I would "milk" several times a day until the dead and damaged tissue was gone and the wound started closing up. I was to administer antibiotics twice a day, and bring Jenny back for follow-up in a week. I had to undergo the humiliation of explaining what had happened to the vet, and my decision to get rid of the dogs. As soon as the goats were home, the dogs were loaded into the truck and taken to the humane society in Flagstaff. Tears flowed as we reminisced about our times with them. Lucky was adopted as a puppy from the vet in Big Bear and right away, outside the vet's office he started chasing the soccer ball with the kids. Flea was adopted from friends who were moving and could not take him with them. He was a perfect match for his rambunctious master, my 15 year old son. It was a heartbreaking introduction to the realities of raising livestock.

My next goats were not quite as cooperative as Jenny. Big red, Jenny's daughter, never did take to being milked. I had to chase her down every time. Whether I tied her, cobbled her or put her in a straight jacket she would fight me for every drop. By the time we were done, the milk would be so filthy it was good for nothing but the chickens. Big Red passed her attitudes on to all her offspring. I never handled Red much as a kid, so as she grew, she became wild. Her kids would follow her everywhere and I could never get close. Sadly, Big Red fell victim to wolf dog attacks, along with her mother, and we lost her for good.

On the flip side, nothing beats wrestling a free ranging goat for possession of a bale of hay. Several bales of good alfalfa were scattered to the winds as my greedy goats binged on them before I could get them put away. I quickly learned to leave a short length of rope on each goat's collar, that I could grab to lead the goat into a stall while I put the hay into the hay shed. That said, we do raise our animals for food. This was the plan anyway, until my daughter decided she couldn't eat anything she "knew". No matter how much I tried to explain to her that it is better to eat meat you knew was raised with love and good food instead of in an unsanitary feed lot with drugs and hormones, she would have none of it. This did not, however, stunt her growth, as she is now nearly six feet tall with healthy proportions.

Once we got the goats properly housed, it was time to move on to the next project: horses.

Horses

Now horses are certainly not what you would think of as homestead necessities. More like a drain on cash, with the copious amounts of hay they consume, as well as keeping them healthy and comfortable. But horses were the main reason we moved out to acreage.

Bandit and Judi

My daughter has been obsessed with horses her entire life. Once, when she was 2 or 3 I went into another room for a few minutes and came back to find the front door wide open and my tiny daughter and her older brother across the street and climbing the fence to get to the neighbors' horses. Needless to say, I performed one of those olympian feats of dash and grab before they could get in any further danger. Fast forward 10 or 12 years. Here we were on our very own 5 acres in the country, with an extra $400 in our pockets. One day, while browsing one of the local papers, I saw an ad for 2 BLM (Bureau of Land Management) wild mustangs, $200 each. Owner doesn't have time to work with them. My daughter's birthday was about 2 weeks prior. We went out to look at them and the rest is history. We asked at the vet if anyone would haul them to our house for us, as we didn't yet have a horse trailer. We went home to put up a small corral and caravanned with our horse hauler to pick them up. Being yet a bit wild, it was an adventure loading them into the trailer. Thankfully, the driver was a little bit of a cowboy, and managed it, with the owner's help. We led our precious cargo to their new home and off-loaded them into our 2 strand of barb-less wire corral. My children spent the entire rest of the night gazing in awe and petting their new best friends.

Now the real fun began. We had created our small paddock with barbless wire (being city slickers, we were horrified at the thought of "cruel" barb-wire). With some stall panels donated by our neighbor, we made a large stall and put the horses, Bandit and Judi, in there for starters. I gave strict instructions to my offspring NOT to let them out until we got at least one more strand of wire around the paddock. So naturally, that is the first thing they did. Immediately the horses circled the small paddock, ducked under the wire and began an exploration of the neighborhood. Luckily, these guys had been in the former owner's round pen for two years and were used to being fed, so when we finally caught up with them, offering carrots and apple slices, Bandit, the large gelding and bottomless pit, willingly followed us back home, with Judi tentatively following behind. We got them back in the stall and immediately proceeded to put up two more strands of wire around the paddock. For the next 3 months, until we moved into the place next door, which already had two large paddocks and a barn in place, I found my children at all hours of the day or night, out with the horses, feeding, mucking, and making friends. By the time it was time to move them, they merely took hold of their halters and walked them to their new home.

Pigs

What homestead would be complete without pigs? We are a family who enjoys pork. Sizzling bacon for breakfast; savory sausage; smoky ham; succulent pork chops; tender, juicy baby back ribs.

Wilbur

From his pink, piggy nose to his curly piglet tail we were in love. Wilbur trusted us. He relished the scraps we gave him. He went for walks on the leash. And the day the butcher came to load him into the trailer of death I made sure I had to work elsewhere and the kids had something else to do. The next time we saw him, he was wrapped for the freezer, and believe me, he didn't stay there long. A happily raised pig makes for delicious meat and Wilbur was absolutely delectable. It was a couple of years before we were able to barter for another piglet and store bought bacon was just never the same. Miss Piggy was an entirely different story…

Miss Piggy

The day Miss Piggy arrived we put her in the pig pen and the first thing she did was dig a hole and get out, tearing across the horses' paddock, and staying just far enough away to frustrate me. But if I had learned anything, it was that most animals have a weakness – food. So after several futile attempts at catching her, I opened the pig pen wide and put a big pile of corn right in the middle and set up watch at the kitchen window. Eventually my porcine commando sidled her way back into the pig pen and I stealthily snuck up and closed the door, confident that I had plugged up all her escape routes. Miss Piggy lived up to her name. She ate ravenously and squawked in between meals. She harbored no friendly intentions toward us whatsoever, and on the day we loaded her into the trailer of death to take her to the butcher, we were smiling. When we next saw her, she was dressed in white freezer paper and she, too, only tarried briefly there. In spite of her unfriendly nature, her meat, too was delicious.

"Scatter some scratch, put scraps in one bowl, more scratch in another, and fill up the water bowl. Gather the eggs and you're done. Unless the chickens get out."

Chickens and Other Fowl Creatures

Obviously the first animal that comes to mind in setting up one's homestead is chickens. Little egg and meat factories that can forage for their own food and reproduce themselves perpetually. Right. Well, we started out with some older hens a friend was culling out of his flock. They were still laying, on their last season, and then we could eat them. Grandpa kindly agreed to trek out and assist with the construction of a coop. I thought this would be an excellent opportunity to keep my oldest son out of trouble for a couple weeks. The result was fantastic. They set the posts in cement, framed, insulated and roofed the henhouse, installed homemade doors to the henhouse and chicken yard, and put in little chicken doors from the house to the yard and large windows with wooden shutters which could be closed in colder weather and opened in the heat of summer. They even hung little nest boxes on the wall. The yard was the coup de grace. It was enclosed in chicken wire from six inches below ground to rooftop and then across the entire top to prevent the chickens from flying the coop, and predators from getting in. Our cats found it particularly amusing to sit on top of the wire and watch the chickens below.

Feeding and watering the chickens is one of the easiest chores. Scatter some scratch, put scraps in one bowl, more scratch in another and fill up the water bowl. Gather the eggs and you're done. Unless the chickens get out. With all the dogs, coyotes and other predators around our area, we never let the chickens out unless we were there to spot trouble. If I had to go to work or somewhere, the chickens had to stay in. Once they were out, they had no intention of returning to the coop until evening feeding and roosting time. Thus, if they escaped, we had to chase them back into the coop or catch them individually and put them back. This happened frequently. I finally decided it was the kids' job to catch them, as they could run much better than I could.

Sheep

Once again, it was my daughter's fault. She wanted a heifer for her 4H project, but after checking into it, I realized that just was not going to happen. Not at $800-$1500 just for the calf. My newfound cousin just happened to have a lamb he needed to get rid of and my dear child quickly changed her project and HAD to have that lamb.

Little Bo Peep

So we got Little Bo Peep and made a pen for her and got lamb milk replacer to bottle feed her. We went to all the 4H classes and did all of the project. We had a shearing day and then came the County Fair.

We loaded BoPeep and all her feed and gear into the truck about 6am on the day we were to bring her to the fairgrounds. My children also had to bring their show clothes, for showing their animals to the judges. In addition to Bo, they were showing chickens and rabbits. So there was quite a bit to haul up to Flagstaff. The fair is held over a long weekend, so we had to travel back and forth from Thursday to Monday. Each day the animals had to be fed, cared for, and groomed. It might have been better to get a campsite, but we didn't. Bo and her mistress did quite well, as did the kids and their other animals. Bo did not do well enough to be placed in the auction, and we were okay with that. We proceeded to take her back home and care for her for many more years.

Llamas – Go Figure!

I first saw a llama at the county fair. I wasn't real excited about it, but noticed that their underwool was soft and luxurious and sold for enormous prices. So later when we found ourselves with too many horses and an opportunity to trade a couple of them for less costly to feed llamas, we jumped on it. I had visions of shearing the thick wool and spinning it for weaving and crocheting. The llamas had other ideas. At first they were friendly and shy. Later the male would charge at us and spit at us if we came near. The female was curious but skittish. They liked to escape their pen and go exploring up the street. I often had to use my friend's golf cart to chase them down and herd them back into their pen. Later on we hired a couple of local kids to help us put a fence up. No more chasing down llamas.

BOOK 2 – MILKING THE WILD GOAT

HOW TO FIND LAND AND SET UP YOUR HOMESTEAD

"Learning to milk a cow was an adventure. I dubbed Mabel the "Dancing Jersey Milk Cow" for good reason."

Marvelous Mabel the Dancing Jersey Milk Cow

It is impossible to explain how I finally acquired a dairy cow without explaining Maryruth. My best friend, kindred spirit, and confidante. I met Maryruth at the Art Guild's 1st annual "Art in the Park" show at the tiny park next to our tiny library and water dept. She was dressed in an 1890's walking dress and handing out samples of homemade cream cheese and (not homemade) crackers. She hollered at me as I pushed my new baby's stroller by and pressed the samples into my hand. We got to talking about milking and cheese and soap. She was selling homemade soaps and I was just starting up my website and had been making soap as well. I don't recall the precise progression from acquaintances to bosom friends, but it seemed the more we talked, the more we had to talk about. She had some health issues and found she no longer wanted <u>all</u> the responsibility of a milk cow, but didn't want to get rid of her either. And so began our co-ownership of Mabel the Marvelous Dancing Jersey Milk Cow. She would keep Mabel up at her place for a few months, be responsible for any vet bills, arrange for "gentleman callers" at a certain time of year, etc. I would help with milking and contribute toward the feed. Then Mabel would come out to my place for a few months and I would do all the milking and buy most of the feed.

BOOK 2 – MILKING THE WILD GOAT

HOW TO FIND LAND AND SET UP YOUR HOMESTEAD

Learning to milk a cow was an adventure. I dubbed Mabel the "Dancing Jersey Milk Cow" for good reason. She is in perpetual motion when you are milking her. At first I would stand next to her, lean against her ample belly and bend over to milk, "dancing" with her. I would also have to hold the milking bucket at the same time. This was exhausting as well as painful in the back. I next tried squatting by her and moving with her (almost like dancing the limbo) while holding the milk bucket, which proved to be even more exhausting in the knees. Finally I tried the milking stool and using both hands to milk, holding the bucket between my feet. This worked out much better and Mabel only stepped on my foot occasionally. More often, she missed and stepped right in the bucket.

Not being one to give up easily, I constructed a crude squeeze, a narrow stall in which a large animal like a horse or cow can be confined for vet check-ups, vaccinations, branding or milking. This worked quite well for milking for several months. During this time I started noticing things. Mabel moves mainly for two reasons – food and flies. As long as she is well supplied with hay and grain and a "can't kick" (a contraption that fits loosely around the hip, preventing free movement of the rear leg), with her head tied to the fence in easy reach of the food, she is perfectly content to stand for milking. Unless she is being eaten by flies. Then she does tend to sway, stomp and swish her tail. I came to realize this when I started doing the same thing (minus the tail). The flies are downright carnivorous!

Nowadays I tie Mabel right in the corral. I try to get out to milk her before the flies wake up. I keep her well supplied with hay and grain while milking, make sure the "can't kick" is properly applied and stay alert to fly stomps and swishes. I move the milking stool as needed as she does tend to change position frequently, and I milk into a small quart size container that I pour into the covered milk bucket, strategically located a safe distance away from our barnyard ballerina.

"Nothing is as cuddly as a newborn kitten, except maybe a puppy. Now I have four lady cats to spay."

Barn Cats

When we moved to our property, we didn't have any cats. As soon as we moved, our old neighbors called to tell us they had our cat. We insisted that our cat had run off and never come back, but they said they had an orange and white cat with a tag and our phone number on it. We explained that we did not have an orange and white cat and that our black cat had run away months ago. Finally we caved in and went to get the cat. He was a beautiful ginger and white tabby who made it a point to inspect everything thoroughly. He kept tabs on us everywhere we went. If something was happening, he had to investigate. We christened him "Sherlock Holmes". Next, one of my coworkers at the restaurant had to get rid of her two cats. Would we take them, just for a little while until she could find a home for them? Guess whose home they found?

Missy was a delicate, short haired feminine feline who was supposed to be fixed. Two litters later we decided she wasn't. Unfortunately, Missy and the second litter disappeared, likely victims of coyotes.

Buster is a fluffy black cat who made fast friends with Sherlock. After ten years, Buster and Sherlock seem to have slowed down on their rodent hunting responsibilities. I found a mouse in the house one winter, and a family of mice in the feed shed. The boys were given a stern talking to. The following summer I found a small snake, a sure sign that the rodent population was increasing. I brought in a succession of stray cats which the boys swiftly ran off. I had pretty much given up on getting a young mouser in when Alina showed up. Some friends couldn't keep her, so I decided to set her up in the barn and keep her in a crate for a couple of weeks until she recognized this place as her new home. In only three days, I was able to let her stay out of the crate. She met and mastered the boys and took over mousing duties. Unfortunately she quickly met the local toms, who happily impregnated her. Nothing is as cuddly as a newborn kitten, except maybe a puppy. Now I have four lady cats to spay.

Goldfish

For years my sons have tried to keep goldfish. They tend to die quickly around here. Apparently we are typical of most goldfish owners – we over feed them. I have never understood this. I always follow the directions on the package. Apparently the pet stores have quite a scam running with the fish food folks and the feeder fish breeders. It goes something like this: Child begs for fish. Parent buys tank, filters, aerators, gravel, fake plants, goldfish, fish medications and fish food. Parent sets up tank, gravel, aerators, filters, fake plants and fish. Child over feeds fish. Fish dies. Parent feeds fish to chickens. Cycle starts over. One day I decided to throw the surviving fish into the goats' water tank. That was three years ago. They're quite large now. They've never been fed anything but whatever they eat in the water tank. The goats favor that particular bucket. Every so often we scoop a fish out for the aquarium in the house. We now have goldfish in about half our water tanks. We continue adding new ones to the tanks that don't have any. Soon they all will.

Wiley Coyote (Predators)

Wolf Dogs

One year, well into our homesteading experience, we had ordered an overload of chicks. As they grew, we separated out the roosters and let them free range and nest in the little fenced yard off the back of our house. One day I noticed some strange dogs coming around the back yard. As we didn't have a dog at the time, I was wondering how long they had been coming around. They seemed very friendly, coming right up to the fence and wagging their tails at me. Then the chickens started disappearing. Slow on the pickup as I am sometimes, we lost nearly the whole flock before I realized what these doggies were up to. When they ran out of easy chicken pickens, the dogs started in on our goat herd. After the first incident of finding a dead, mangled goat in the goat pen, and a dog frantically climbing the fence to get out, we removed all items that a dog could use to jump into the pen and called animal control. We put the mommas and babies in what we thought would be a more secure stall under the barn. We lined the stall with "pig" panels of heavy gauge wire. A few mornings later, I awoke once again to screaming goats. I looked out the window and saw a black doglike shape next to the new goat stall. I grabbed my pistol and quickly made my way outside. Inexplicably, the dog went on with whatever he was doing until I was nearly upon him. Trembling, I clicked off the safety, pointed the pistol at the black mass and pulled the trigger. A yelp, a flash and the dog was gone, leaving a trail of blood. I examined the situation and found that one of the goats' legs had been pulled right through the heavy gauge wire 3"x3" square, and gnawed on by the dog, while the other end of said goat desperately screamed for help. She was my first and favorite milker. Jenny. The leg was a stringy mass of blood and cartilage. I put her down.

Calls to animal control brought little satisfaction. The dogs were actually wolf hybrids - not bound by the leash law because they were "wild" animals. Not against the law to breed, because they were half dog. It was a no-win situation. The officer left me a couple of traps, which I baited, and caught one of the dogs. When the officer lifted the trap into his truck, the dog tried to escape and broke the trap. The escape was unsuccessful, but the broken trap was blamed on me!

Now I really felt like I was living in the wild west. I drove up to Flagstaff and invested in a lightweight .22 rifle and some ammunition, and went home to practice. The next dog that came to the smorgasbord never made it home. The rifle also helped keep the coyotes at bay. Even though they tend to run off at the first sound of a door opening, I have found that the loud noise of firing off a shot will send them looking for easier pickin's for quite some time.

Death on the Homestead

Death, as well as life, is a frequent visitor to the homestead. Sometimes the death of our animals leaves us bereaved.

Princess

Princess was such an animal. I have had a steady procession of dogs through my life, but three hold a very special place. Kimba, a purebred poodle and my very first puppy, acquired when I was age 5. He died at 8 years old. Benson, a purebred cocker spaniel, my wedding gift to my husband. I took custody of Benson in the divorce. Benson died at the ripe old age of sixteen.

Princess is the latest. She arrived as a puppy my best friend knew was meant for me. She was a ginger colored Australian Kelpie mix, born on the Navajo Reservation and acquired by Maryruth when she was doing a special event for the radio station for the blind that she volunteered at. A Navajo man was outside the store where the event was taking place, with a box of puppies and one kept catching Maryruth's eye. How she talked me into it I'll never know, my latest dog had just died of parvo and I was not ready for more heartbreak. But that night Princess lay tucked in a shoebox next to my bed, because I insisted she was too small to stay outside. As she grew, we got all her shots, got her spayed and took her everywhere. She never barked. She buried her poop like a cat. At least I think she did, I never caught her and never found any of her feces. She hunted mice and birds and kept other dogs and coyotes away. One day a coyote went after one of our turkeys and she chased off the coyote and herded the turkey back. She was great at herding the chickens, but when it came to the goats, sheep and horses she would disappear. We think a couple of kicks from a horse may have made her wary of the larger animals.

Princess loved to go everywhere with us. She would hop in the truck and when we got home she was first out, making the rounds of the homestead. One day I had borrowed Maryruth's car and let her use my truck. When I got home with the truck I realized I still had her car keys. So we loaded back up in the truck with Princess and dropped off Maryruth's keys. We arrived home exhausted. Princess did not come in that night. We walked around calling for her then finally went in to bed. Worried, in the morning I called and searched for her again. No sign. Finally, about 5p.m., after a 100-plus degree day, I got a sick feeling in my stomach and went and checked the truck. My wonderful, beautiful dog, who never barked or whined, stumbled out. I carried her to the house and checked her temperature. When the mercury reached 108 degrees I pulled the thermometer out and put Princess in a cold bath. She took some water but no food. I kept bathing her and holding her, begging her to hang on. She seemed to perk up and wanted to go outside. She found a cozy little area under the house and wouldn't come out. We had to crawl in to get her. She fought hard, but after a week she succumbed. I buried several shards of my heart with her. I still miss the comfort of her laying on my feet in front of the fire, and her romps through the woods while we collected fodder for our woodstove. I still marvel that she would catch and eat a raven that would attack my lambs and rabbits, yet keep watch over a baby chicken who had strayed out of the cage, until I arrived to replace it. In the two short years she was with us, she burrowed deeply into our hearts.

More to Life

County Fair

The Coconino County Fair is a very rural event. Unlike the Los Angeles (California) County Fair, which greatly resembles Disneyland as far as parking, rides (and pictures) too numerous to count, paved animal stalls, and massive competition, the Coconino county Fair, held in Flagstaff is a really enjoyable, down home event. The midway is big enough to entertain the teenagers without detracting from the main event. The barns have dirt floors with plenty of straw bedding. Real 4H and FFAers groom and milk and collect eggs from animals bred locally. Real ranch kids show their steers. Local grocers try to outbid each other at the 4H/FFA auction. The "buyer's breakfast" sees future farmers and ranchers selling the benefits of their particular animals to buyers from Safeway, local markets, and big ranchers.

Exhibit halls overflow with locally produced pies and cakes, quilts and beadwork, artwork from the schools, projects made by the children, farm and garden produce, and locally grown flowers. The local train club tweaks their exhibit every year with some new special effect, and encourages new enthusiasts. A mini water-barrel choo-choo train snakes through food stands and vendor booths. Amid the cacophony, we would camp with other 4H families at the adjacent campground, arriving at the fairgrounds long before opening, chatting with carnies from the midway, food and other vendors as they sip coffee, propping heavy eyelids open, setting up for another day of lively crowds. Then back to the barns to feed, water, groom and clean stalls. All before the fair opens to the public for the day. It's a peaceful and intimate time.

Later, we might volunteer at an exhibit or hang out at the animal barns to answer questions. Volunteering is a good way to get into the fair for free. The work is pleasant, usually just a couple of hours, and the rest of the day is yours to enjoy the fair. In some exhibits, children over a certain age can also volunteer and get free entry. 4H and FFA members with animals in the fair are admitted to tend to their animals.

The Neighbors

When we first set up our camp, it was novel to let our shepherd mix and our rottweiler run around the property. Five acres seemed so big. Unfortunately, it wasn't fenced, and they soon discovered the neighbors' horses. I was blissfully ignorant of the implications of this until I watched them chasing the horses one day. They were nipping at their feet. I suddenly had a moment of clarity and called the dogs back. With a growing shame at my ignorance, I put the dogs on long chains around the trees and began constructing a dog run. My daughter began going over to admire the horses and was soon invited to ride. The next thing I knew, she was feeding and caring for the horses whenever the neighbors went away for a few days.

"The kids got involved in 4H, where we became friends with people who were living the way we wanted to."

4H

The kids got involved in 4H, where we became friends with people who were living the way we wanted to. 4H was started as a way for universities in rural areas to get their ideas of how to improve farming and animal husbandry methods out to the new generation. The idea has stuck and grown to include homemaking, forestry, and many other rural business applications. Now, "4H is the nation's largest positive youth development and mentoring organization", according to their website, 4-h.org, which also explains that "the 4 H's are Head, Heart, Hands, and Health, and are the 4 values that members work on through fun and engaging programs". Another similar organization is FFA or Future Farmers of America.

My children started out with rabbits and chickens and some of the same people in and leading these groups also raised horses, goats and sheep. Many of these families also homeschooled, so many of our 4H friends served as our homeschool support group as well. We had our weekly meetings at the various leaders' homes so we got a close up look at building with what's available. Scavenged fencing and posts as well as other useful building materials such as paneling and scraps of 2x4s and 2x6s would start out in a designated area known as the "bone yard". As uses were found for these items, they were transformed into animal enclosures, wood pallet gates, and other homestead structures. Several wood pallets might make a small shed for chickens to hide in from sun and rain. Square plastic cat litter buckets became nest boxes for chickens to lay eggs in or rabbits to raise their kits in. An old 55 gallon steel drum might be vented near the bottom to burn trash, with a hardware cloth "spark arrester" over the top. Plastic drums would become feeders for horses, water troughs, or rain barrels, depending on how good condition they were in. Same with old fiberglass or cast iron bath tubs. One friend set a claw foot tub up on rocks, filled it with rain water and would then proceed to light a fire under it whenever she wanted a nice relaxing soak in the hot tub, under the stars. Another family bought an old forestry cabin at auction for $300, and hauled it to their property where they set it on a foundation they dug and poured themselves. They moved in and proceeded to make it into a cozy home. The ideas and possibilities seemed endless.

Some friends were skilled at gardening in the harsh high desert environment. They showed us how to mix in manure and make compost to enrich the non-productive volcanic clay soil. Seeds were planted in basins which would catch and hold precious water instead of letting it run off. Shade cloth and other coverings were used to protect growing plants from the searing hot sun and the desiccating winds. Care had to be taken so rare rains could reach the growing plants.

And no matter what, a little miracle grow always comes in handy. We learned about proper housing and building with what we had available.

"The first time I attended church at St. Anne's I was heartily greeted by a smiling white-haired woman at the entrance to the church. It was a "welcome home, come on in and make yourself comfortable, so glad to see you" greeting. I kept coming back."

Church

One of the main attractions of Ash Fork was the little Catholic Mission, St. Anne's. I had been away from the church for several years but now felt a strong need to return. The first time I attended church at St. Anne's I was heartily greeted by a smiling white-haired woman at the entrance to the church. It wasn't a "polite-hmmm-stranger" greeting. It was a "welcome home, come on in and make yourself comfortable, so glad to see you" greeting. I kept coming back.

One Sunday a month, after Mass, the church ladies provided coffee and donuts and wonderful homemade burritos. The social interaction became the highlight of my week. Not so much for my teenage children.

Each Sunday, after Mass, Religious Education classes were held. As I waited in the back of the church for my children, I felt drawn to the organ. One Sunday I surreptitiously sat behind it and turned it on. I kept the pedal on low and began puttering around on it. I was caught. All of a sudden, I was playing the organ for Mass when the main organist was out of town. Soon, she relocated and I had the (volunteer) job all to myself. This became a lifesaver for me. I became a valuable member of the community and made a valuable contribution with music. I loved playing every week and made some friends that I would not otherwise have made.

"After every game, the boys would pile into the back of coach's pickup and we would all drive through town so they could shout at the top of their lungs "undefeated Cubs, undefeated Cubs!" Only in a small town..."

Baseball

Baseball, on the other hand, was a highlight for my youngest son. He loved the game and he loved the interaction. The throwing, hitting and catching was an activity where he could shine. He took great pleasure in our games of catch, seeing how hard he could throw until mom's hand was too sore to catch anymore.

The last year he played, his team, the Cubs, won the championship in their division. After every game, the boys would pile into the back of coach's pickup and we would all drive through town so they could shout at the top of their lungs "undefeated Cubs, undefeated Cubs!" Only in a small town…

Conclusion

The great homesteading adventure continues. The place is a work in progress. At this time we are embarking on another adventure which will put us homesteading on the road quite a bit. But the old place is not forgotten and there are still plans to continue with improvements for sustainable living and a more permanent return some day. Right now I'm trying to figure out how to travel in a ten foot trailer with two adults, an active boy, a pit bull, two laying hens and a milk goat…

Resources for More Info

Websites: note – if link doesn't work, try to copy and paste into your address bar.

Mrs. D's Homestead – my website and blog, where I write about our adventures from moving out of the city, to setting up and running our homestead, to transitioning to full-time rving/roadsteading. http://www.mrsdshomestead.com.

Homesteading With Mrs. D – my Grit Magazine reader blog. Here I post other items of interest about homesteading.
http://www.grit.com/blogs/homesteading-with-mrs
-d.aspx

Grit Magazine – monthly print and online magazine with all kinds of info on homesteading, small farming and rural living. Lots of reader blogs from people actually living the life. http://www.grit.com/

Nourishing Days – a young family's story of living off-grid, gardening and making from scratch in Texas. http://www.nourishingdays.com/

Backwoods Home Magazine – print and online magazine with lots of "practical ideas for self-reliant living". http://www.backwoodshome.com/

Floyd Family Homestead – one family's story of moving back to the land. Lots of tips and diy info. https://www.floydfamilyhomestead.com/

Rural Living Today – tons of resources and articles to help you learn about homesteading, farming and ranching. http://rurallivingtoday.com/rural-living-today/

Weed 'em and Reap – info on urban farming, goats, health and recipes. http://www.weedemandreap.com/

Hillbilly Housewife – my go-to site for cooking from scratch. Lots of tips on menu planning, homemade mixes, homemade convenience foods, and great, simple recipes. http://www.hillbillyhousewife.com/

So Sew Easy – free patterns, tutorials and instructions for beginning sewists. http://so-sew-easy.com/

Books: All books available on Amazon as of date of this writing.

Back to Basics: How To Learn and Enjoy Traditional American Skills, by Reader's Digest

The classic guide to self-sufficiency. Includes projects, recipes, and background info on everything from setting up the homestead, raising and butchering animals, tanning hides, gardening, soapmaking, etc.

https://www.amazon.com/Back-Basics-Traditional-American-Skills/dp/0895770865/ref=sr_1_2?s=books&ie=UTF8&qid=1472501866&sr=1-2&keywords=back+to+basics

The Encyclopedia of Country Living, by Carla Emery

Another classic resource from the '70s. Everything for sustainable living on the homestead: animals, food, cooking on a woodstove, how to milk a goat, and more.

https://www.amazon.com/Encyclopedia-Country-Living-40th-Anniversary-ebook/dp/B007WL0JUQ/ref=sr_1_2?s=books&ie=UTF8&qid=1472501937&sr=1-2&keywords=homesteading+self+sufficiency#nav-subnav

DIY Projects for the Self-Sufficient Homeowner: 25 Ways to Build a Self-Reliant Lifestyle, by Betsy Matheson

Published in 2011, this book also includes projects for solar, hydro, and utility back-up systems.

https://www.amazon.com/DIY-Projects-Self-Suffici ent-Homeowner-Self-Reliant-ebook/dp/B0052XSEKI /ref=sr_1_11?s=books&ie=UTF8&qid=1472501937& sr=1-11&keywords=homesteading+self+sufficiency#n av-subnav

More With Less Cookbook, by Doris Janzen Longacre

Classic cookbook, advocating a diet with more whole grains, vegetables, and fruits, less meat, saturated fats, and sugars. Hundreds of recipes and lots of nutritional info.

https://www.amazon.com/More---Less-Cookbook-World-Community-ebook/dp/B00AKHQ7N2/ref=sr_ 1_1?s=books&ie=UTF8&qid=1472502053&sr=1-1&k eywords=more+with+less+cookbook#nav-subnav

The Good Life: Helen and Scott Nearing's Sixty years of Self-Sufficient Living, by Helen and Scott Nearing

The Nearings left the city for the country in 1932 and began a homesteading, self-sufficient lifestyle that lasted the rest of their lives. They wrote about and shared their methods and philosophy with all who were interested. This book is the fascinating first part of their story.

https://www.amazon.com/Good-Life-Nearings-Self-Sufficient-Living/dp/0805209700/ref=sr_1_1?s=books&ie=UTF8&qid=1472502331&sr=1-1&keywords=the+good+life+helen+and+scott+nearing%27s+sixty+years+of+self-sufficient+living

The Working Parent's Guide to Homeschooling, by Robyn Dolan

Not a guide to homesteading, just a shameless plug for my other book. It is what it says, take a look.

The Working Parent's Guide to Homeschooling: Tools and Resources for Working Parents to Homeschool, by Robyn Dolan

You Tube Channels of Interest

Mrs. D's Homestead – my You Tube Channel where I post videos about homesteading, homeschooling, simple living; full-time rving; handmade soaps, lotions and folkcrafts.
https://www.youtube.com/user/mrsdshomestead/videos

The Do It Yourself World - a collection of experiments in survival, foraging, off grid living, electronics and alternate energy.
https://www.youtube.com/user/techman2015/videos

Homestead Blessings – the West Ladies' homestead and homespun projects.
https://www.youtube.com/user/HomesteadBlessings/videos

LDS Prepper – homesteading, gardening, solar cooking, and more.
https://www.youtube.com/user/LDSPrepper/videos

Saving Dinner – menu planning, cooking from scratch, weight loss, healthy eating, family dinners.
https://www.youtube.com/user/SavingDinner/vide

<u>os</u>

Simple Solar Homesteading – off-grid homesteader, ideas for simple, sustainable living, solar energy.
https://www.youtube.com/user/solarcabin/videos

Off Grid with Doug and Stacy – moved from city to country in 2011. Living off grid with no solar or wind power, no city water or well. Sustainable living, growing vegetables and meat.
https://www.youtube.com/user/growinginfaithfarm/videos

Can you Help me, Please?

I hope you have enjoyed Get Out of the City and Thrive - Book 2: Milking the Wild Goat – or – How to Set up Your Homestead, as much as I enjoyed writing it.

I would be so grateful if you would leave a review on my website at http://mrsdshomestead.com/site/shop/books-n-down loads/escape-the-city-and-thrive/

In return, if you will leave me your email address on any of my webpages in the newsletter sign up box, I will keep you updated about new book releases, free downloads, quick tips for homesteading, homeschooling and simple living and my latest blog posts, all in one weekly-or-so newsletter!

GET OUT OF THE CITY AND THRIVE!

BOOK 2 – MILKING THE WILD GOAT

HOW TO FIND LAND AND SET UP YOUR HOMESTEAD

About the Author

Robyn Dolan escaped the city for the first time in 1986, as a young mother, with her second child on the way. The family moved to Big Bear Lake, CA and lived and sold Real Estate there among the tall pines, deep lake and hordes of skiers for 12 years.

After her divorce, Ms. Dolan decided to move even farther out and eventually settled in Ash Fork, Arizona, "50 miles from everywhere", west of Flagstaff and north of Prescott. Here she raised goats, sheep, chickens, horses, dogs, cats, the occasional pig, and a milk cow, for another 14 years. She also gave birth to her 4th child in Arizona.

Presently, the author is living full time in her 26 foot travel trailer, traveling between elderly grandpas and enjoying the sights in between. She calls her continuing attempts at homesteading and frugal living "roadsteading" and her son's homeschooling experience "roadschooling".

GET OUT OF THE CITY AND THRIVE!

BOOK 2 – MILKING THE WILD GOAT

HOW TO FIND LAND AND SET UP YOUR HOMESTEAD

www.ingramcontent.com/pod-product-compliance
Lightning Source LLC
Chambersburg PA
CBHW031128250726
48655CB00002B/566